About Face

Story and Illustrations
by
Tonia Colleen Martin

Graphic Design by
Jennifer Rose
Triebwasser

What happened was a mistake, completely unintentional. When people with poor eyesight mingle with those with selective hearing, accidents happen.

The blow flew out of nowhere slamming against her right temple. Sudden as well as quick, shock waves radiated to the place ineptly referred to as the heart, not the vessel of ventricles and veins, but the immutable core of her foundation.

The sting of the blow distorted her vision. In the melee, she assumed a loss of face. Acting upon what she thought was true, made it true. In such cases, mirrors prove useless.

The loss of her face affected everyone and everything.

If you stop and think about it, the whole world suffers in the wake of lost faces.

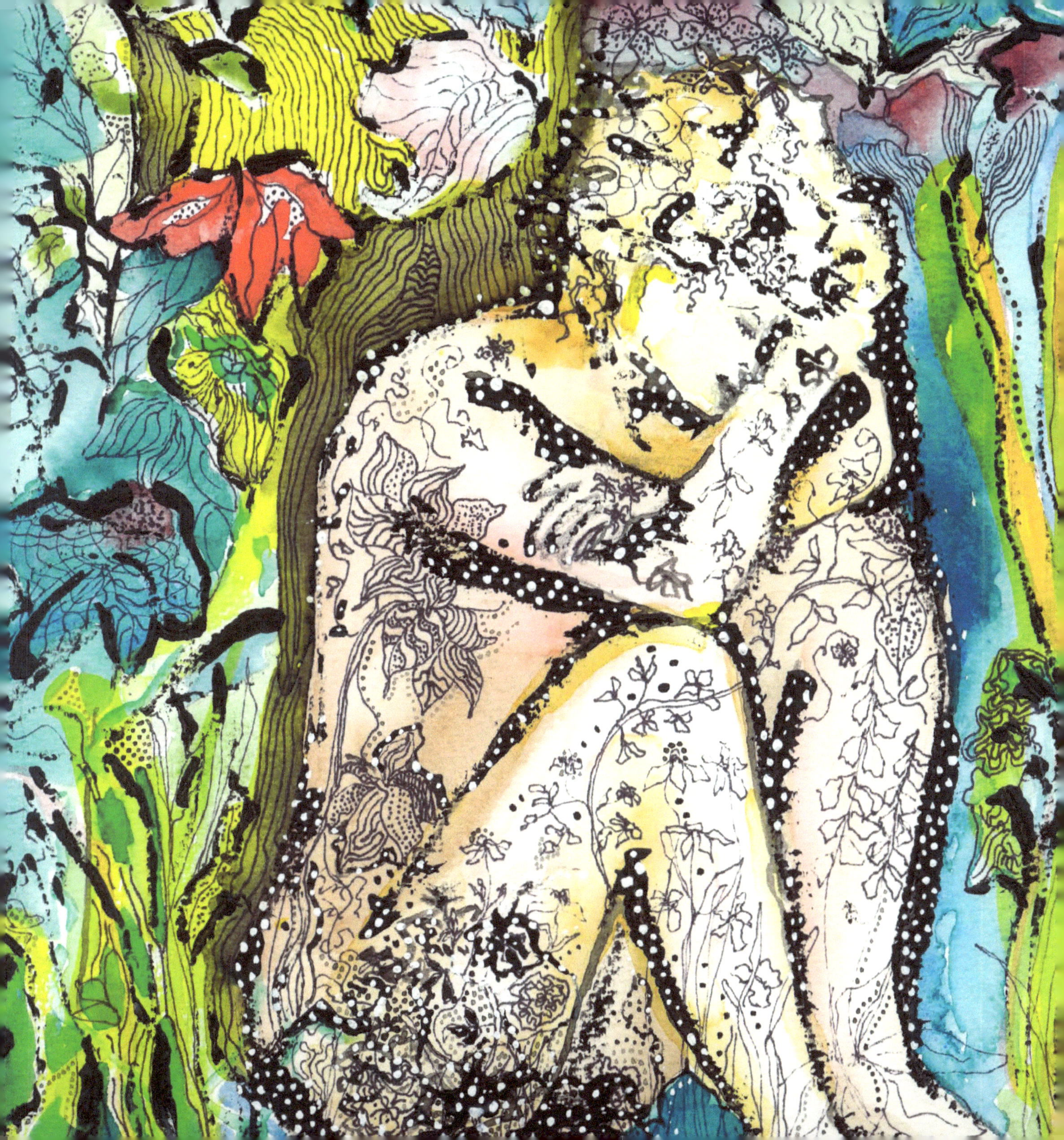

Her search was one of seasons
out of order. Of Summers protesting.

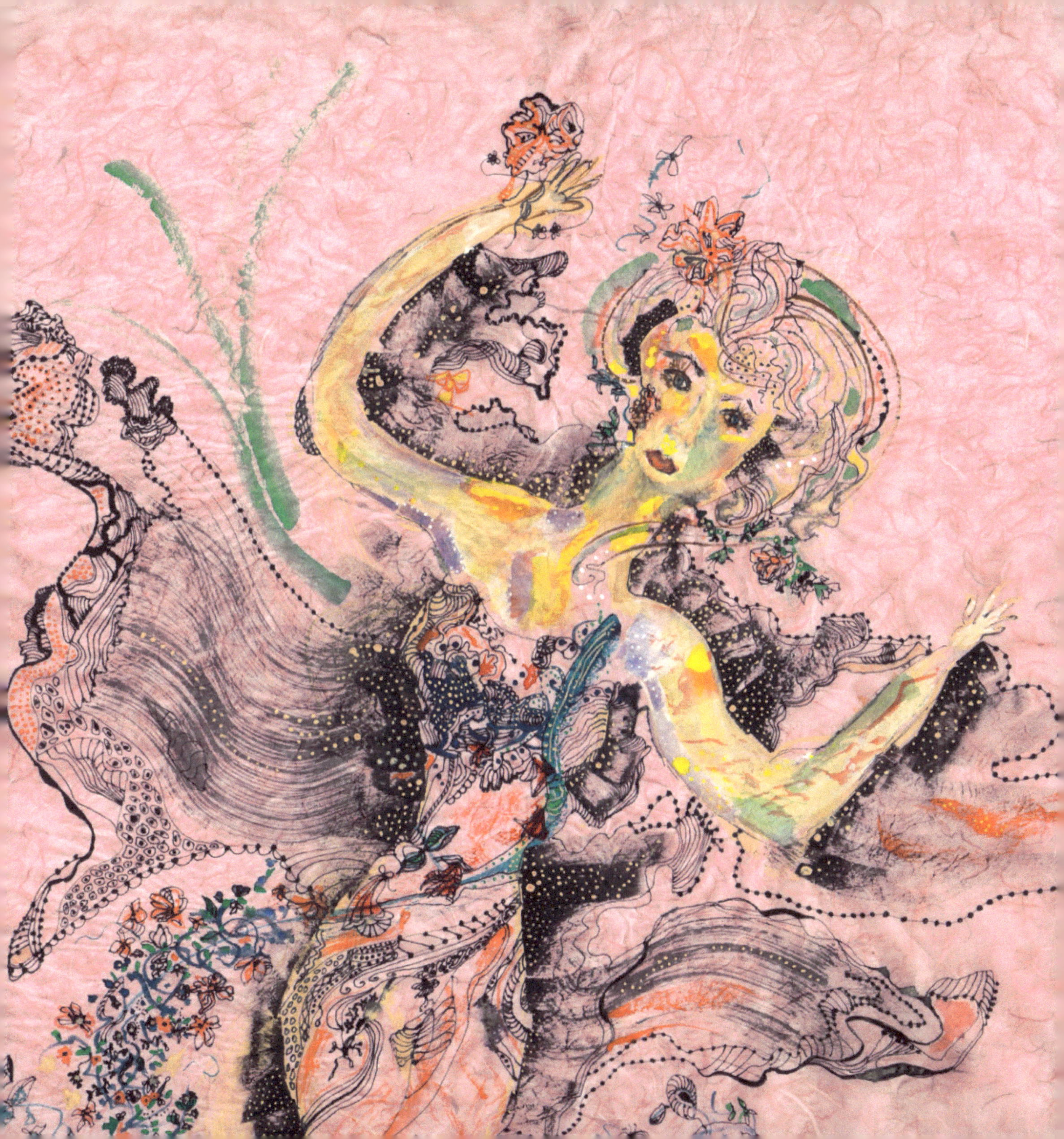

Of Winters resisting.

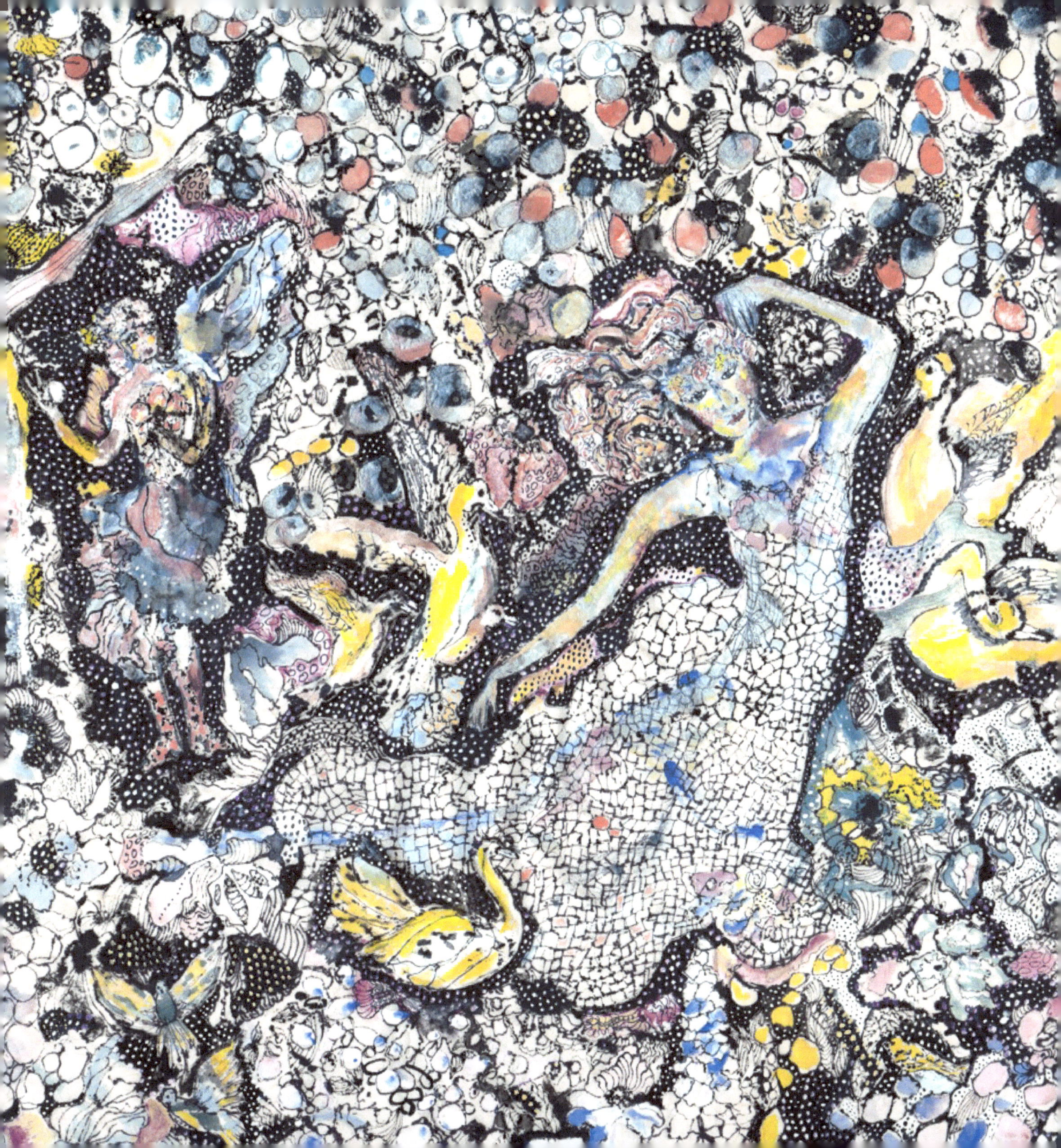

Of Autumns reluctantly waving.

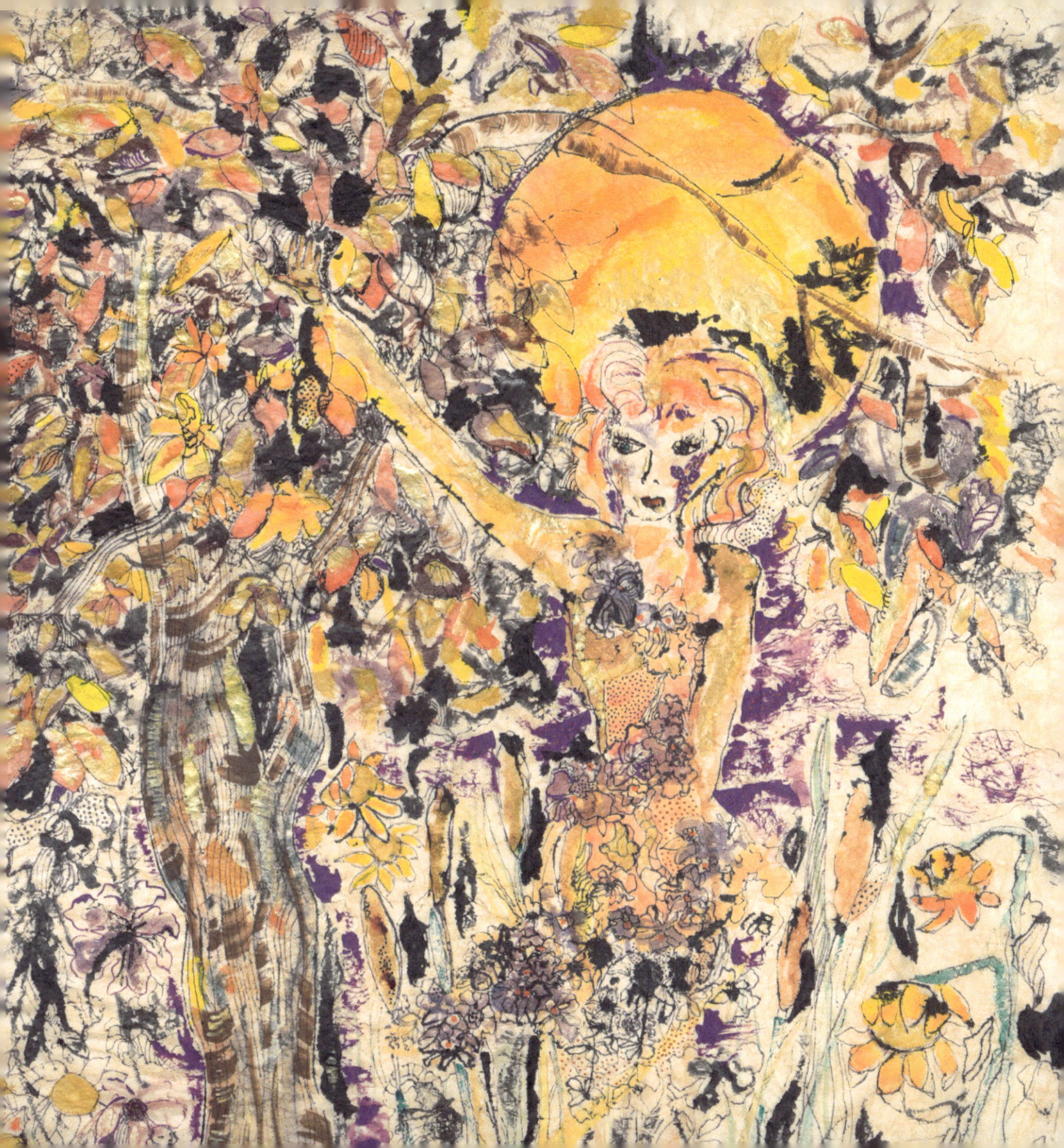

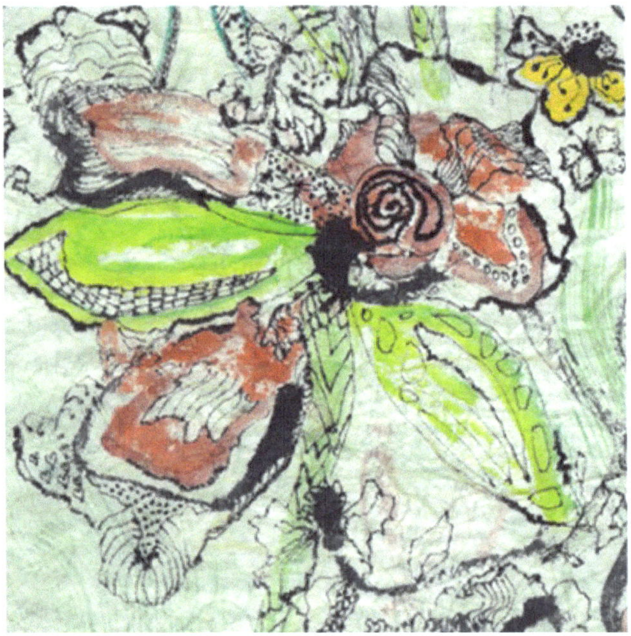

Although Spring came
and went with its compelling
colors, the time of its arrival and the
stint of its stay remained a curious
gamble.

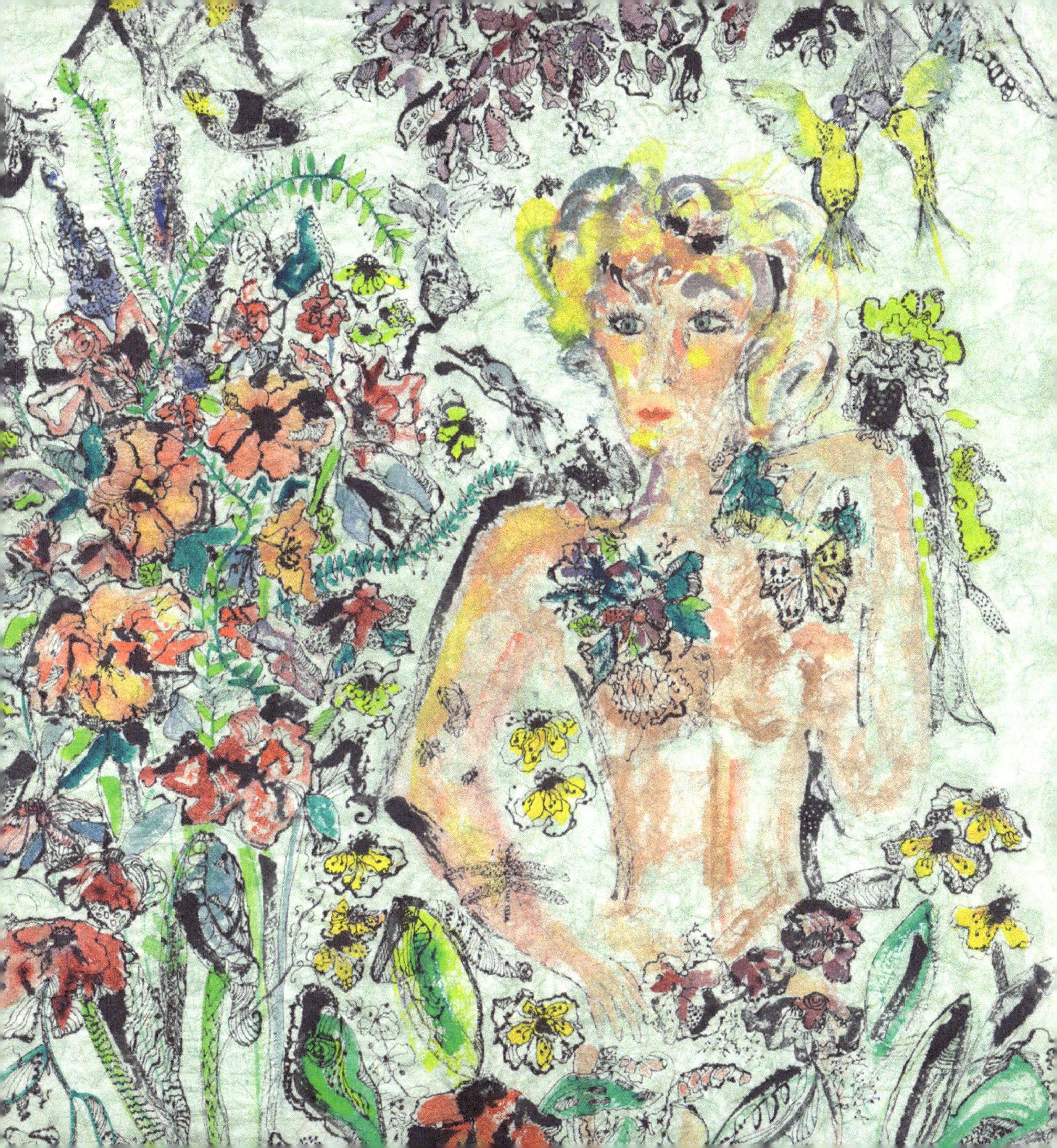

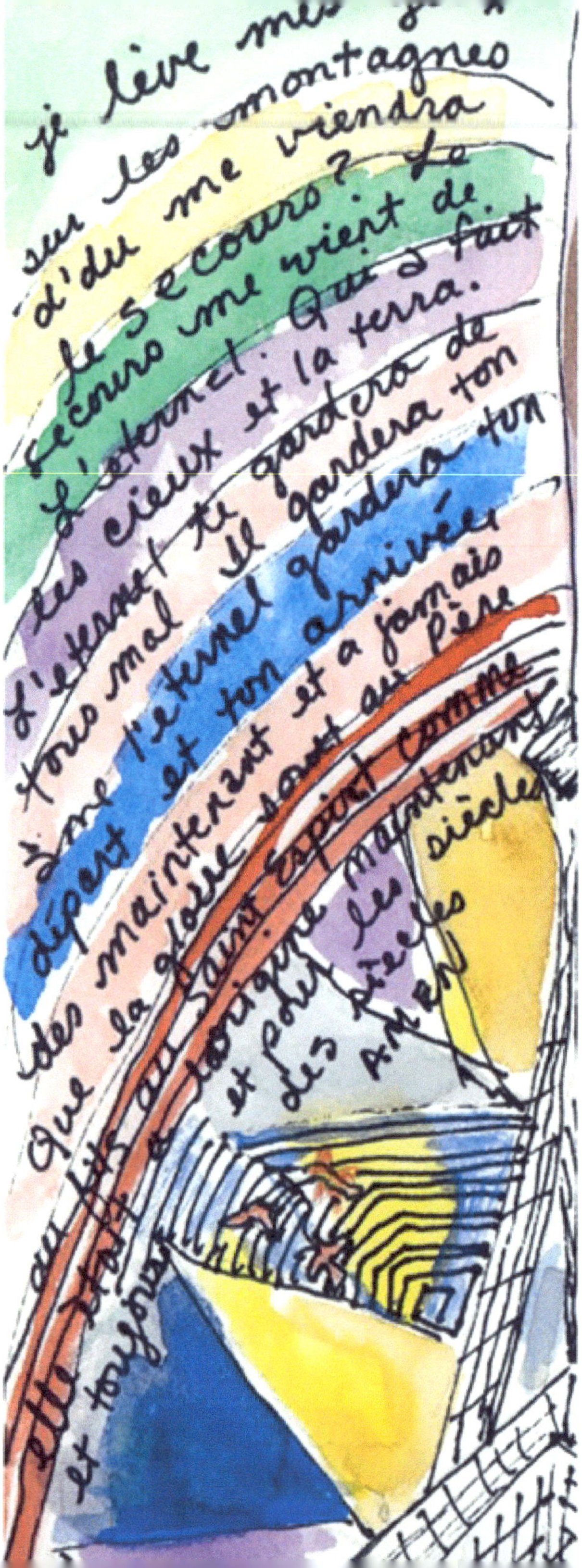

Years passed. In their passing, she forgot what she once knew.

The pain of misremembering plagued her. She numbed herself as best she could and lived in a place of befriending dreams. They tried to inform her, to show her the true shape of her face.

But so much time passed in the absence of her knowing, she could not recognize what she too long misremembered.

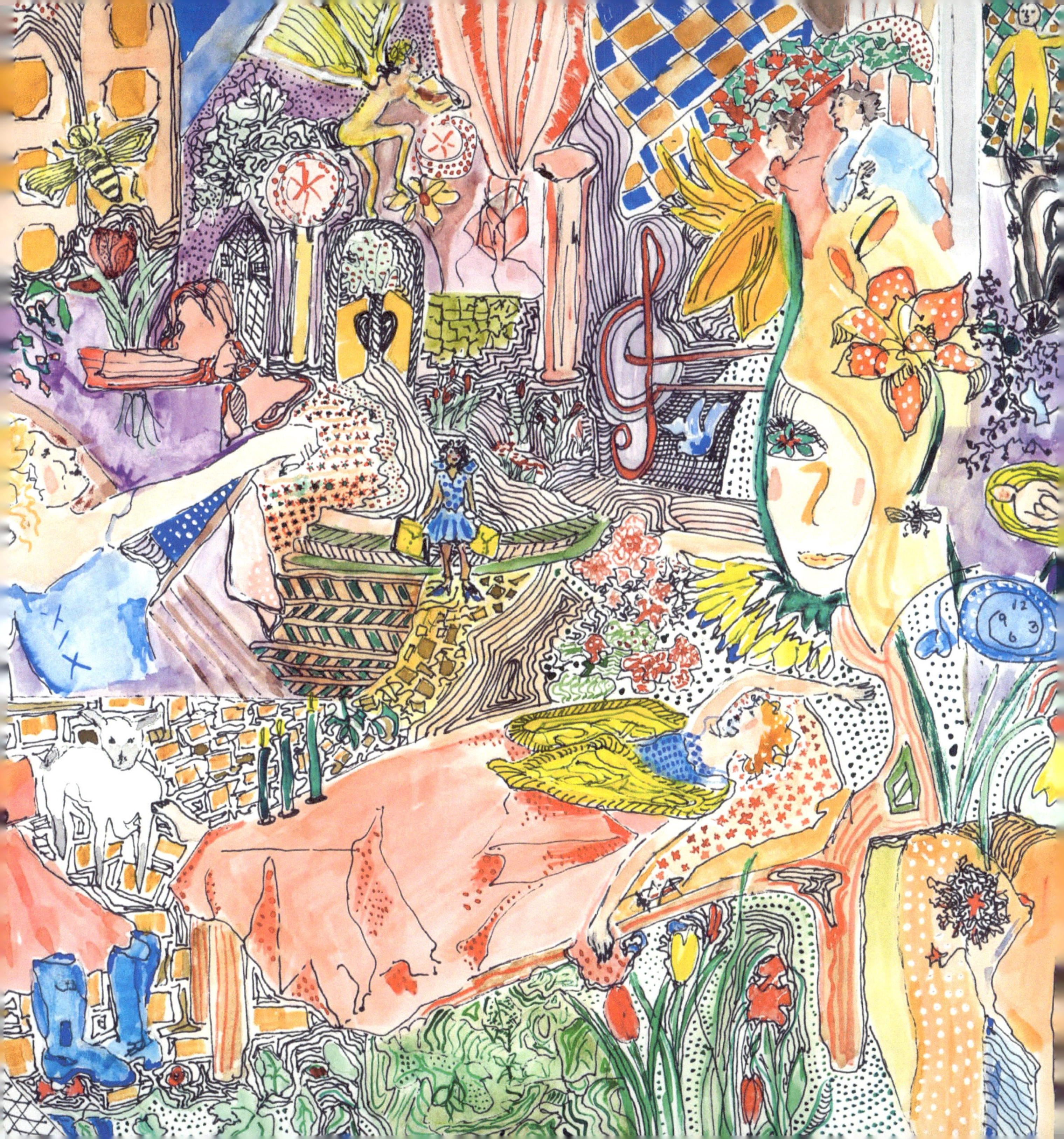

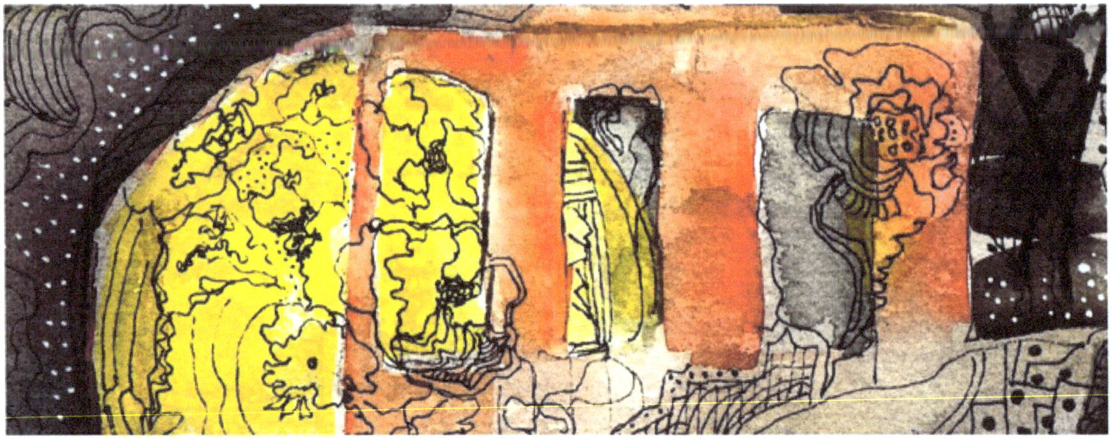

One day she happened upon Hush, Shush and Silence. Old friends, they arrived out of nowhere. The three of them - naked and unassuming. At first, they pointed her away from herself and then they turned her around. They told her what she didn't remember forgetting.

"You did not conceive yourself - neither did your mother, nor your father. You arrived by way of your mother, by way of your father, but God called and breathed you into being."

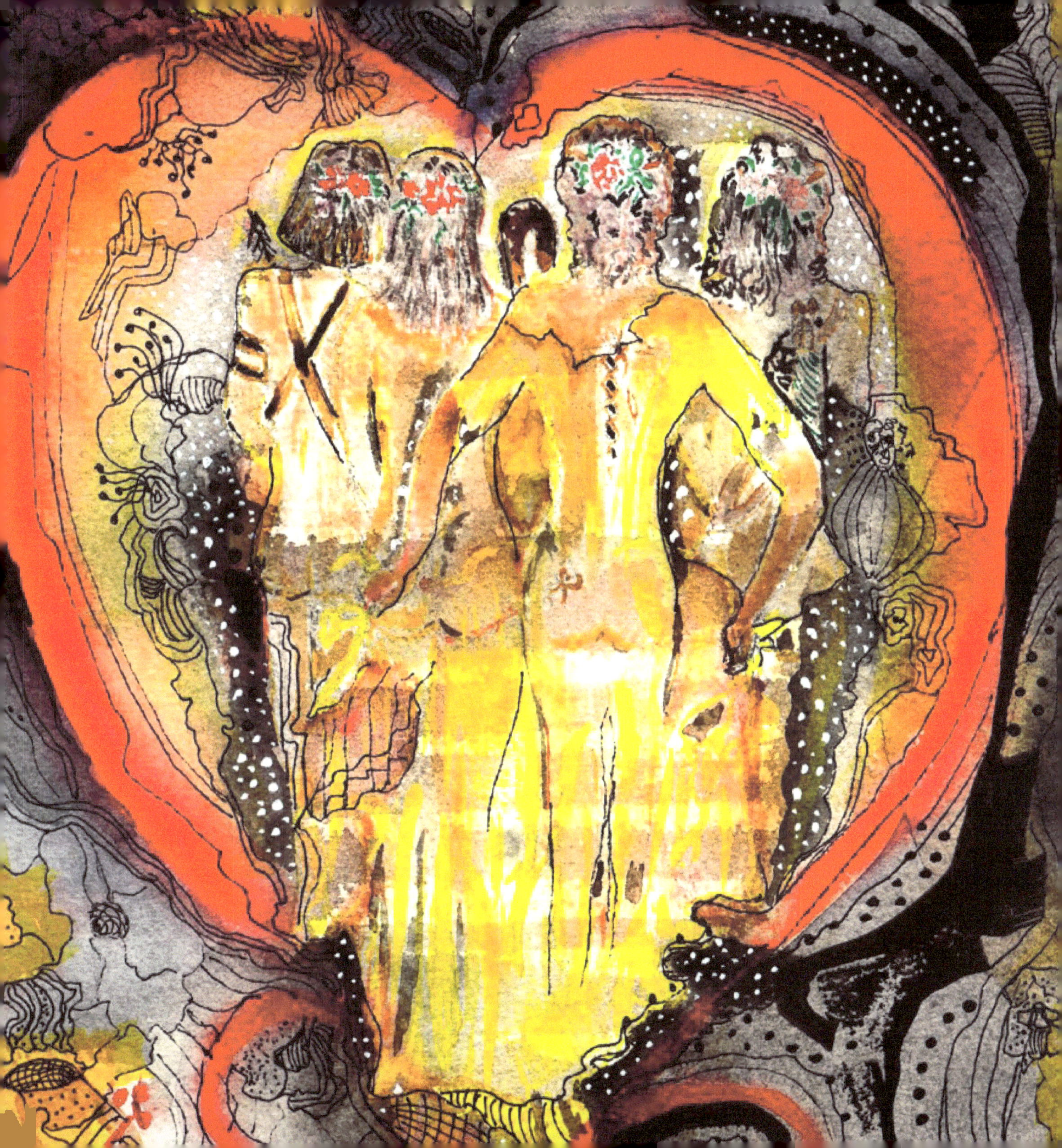

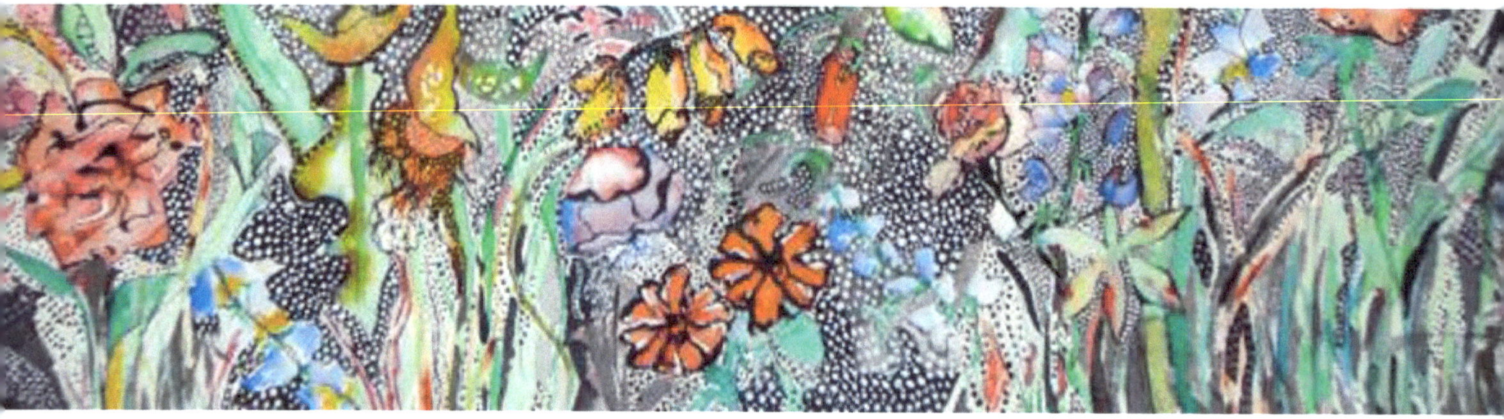

These words brought her to her knees. Collapsing in a pool of tears, she saw her forgotten face. She appeared more beautiful and marred than she imagined.

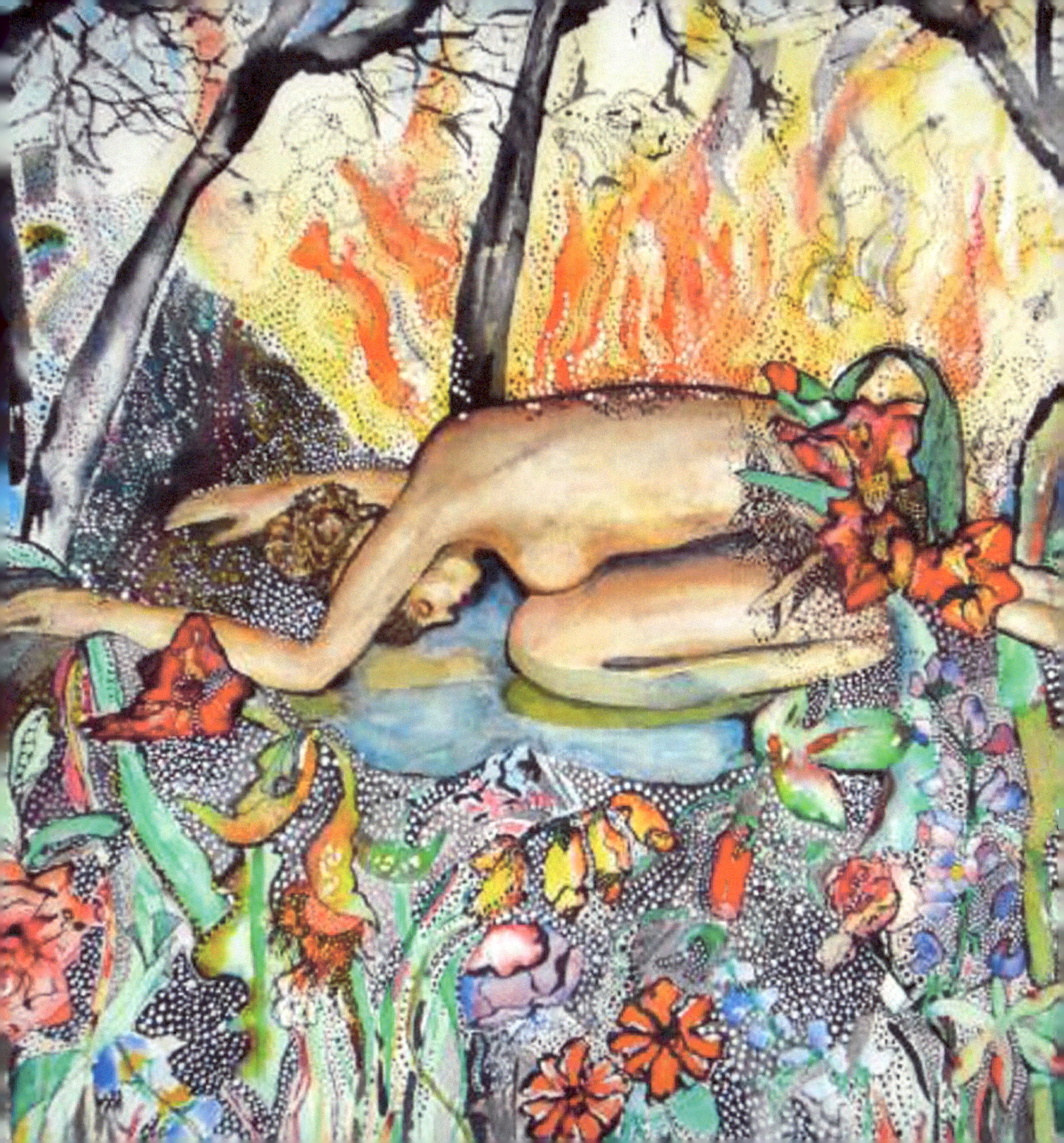

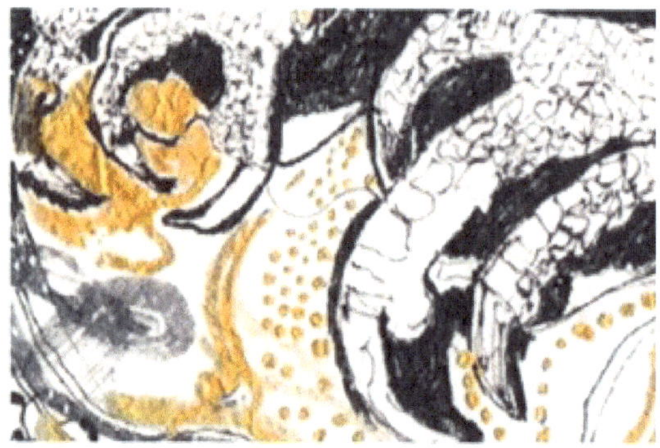

This was a snatching moment, a moment of rapture. A moment of everything being restored. First and foremost, her view of God and next the view of herself. Once she saw God truly, her previously warped view held no sway.

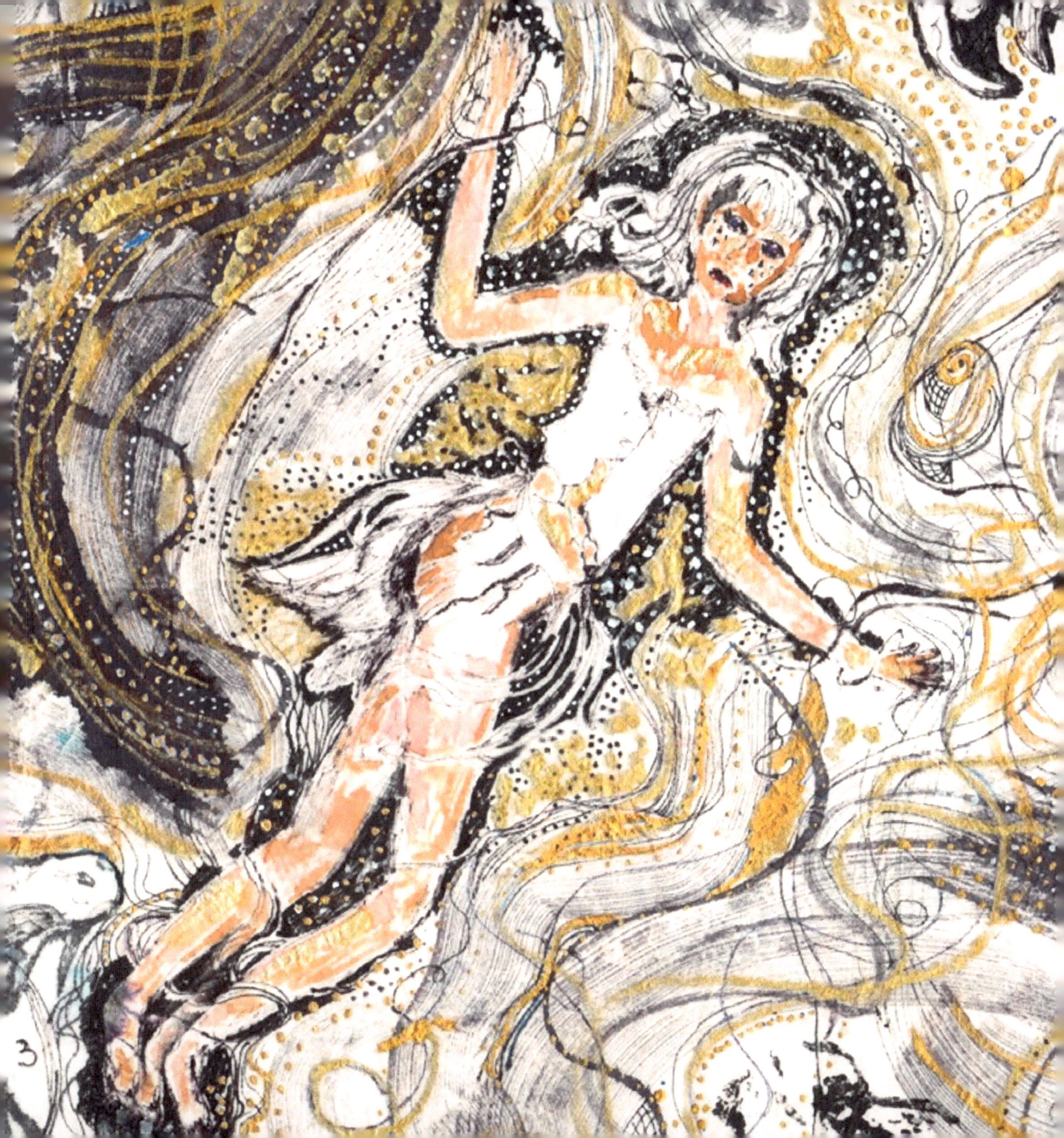

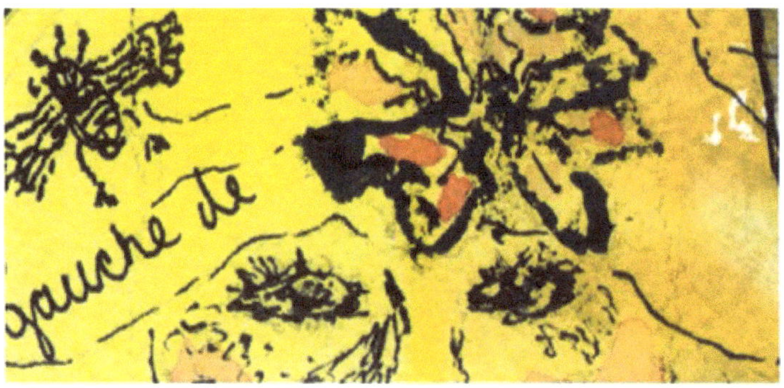

And then she saw other things, darkness and things resplendent in the light. She saw simple things and things complex beyond all questions.

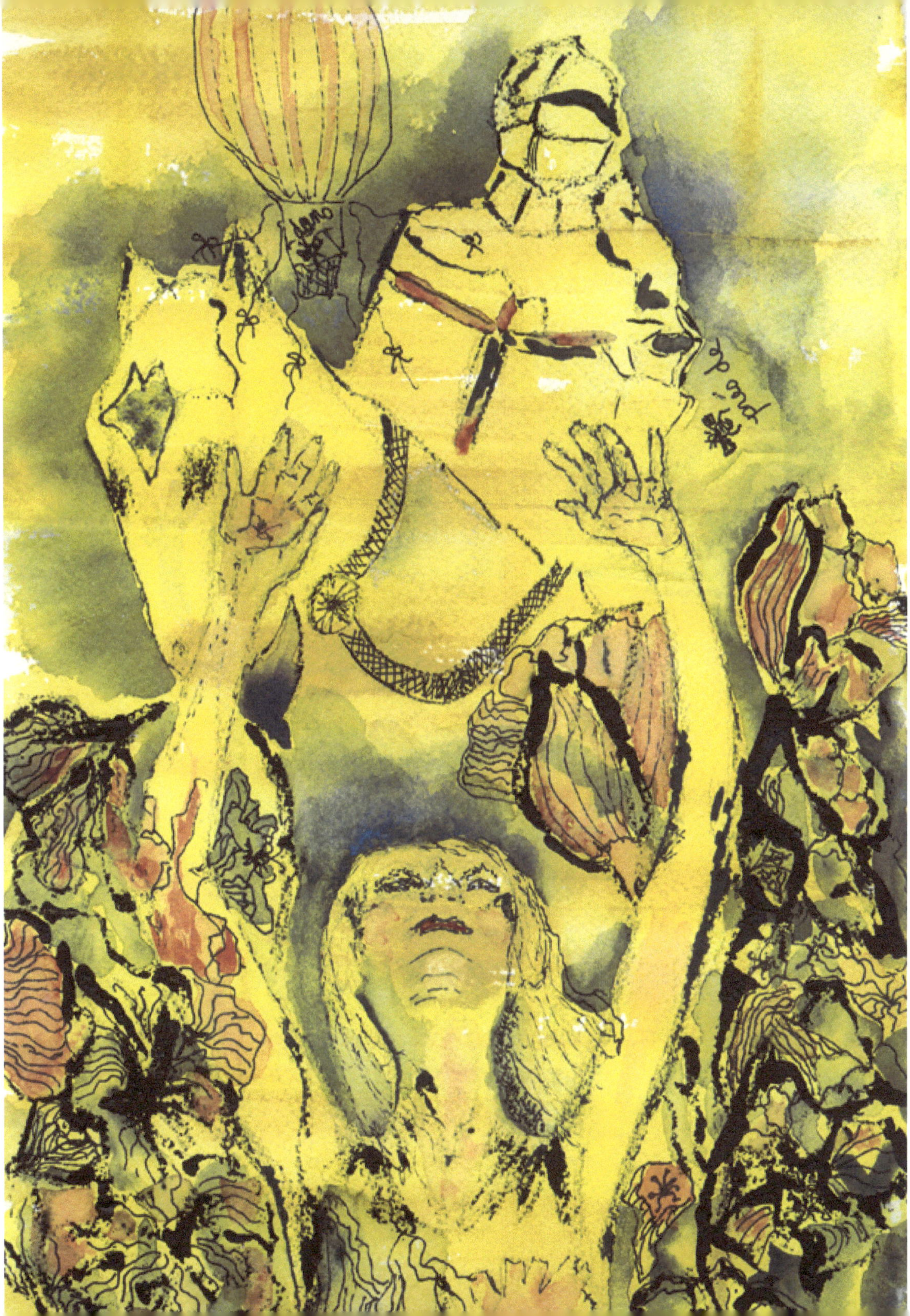

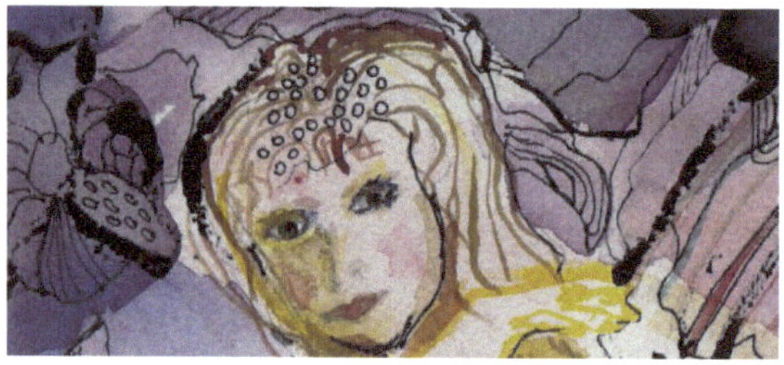

Such sight provided inexplicable wings. Suddenly, she became a woman of triplicate choice. She could either choke on her freedom, languish beneath it or allow herself to be launched beyond the known.

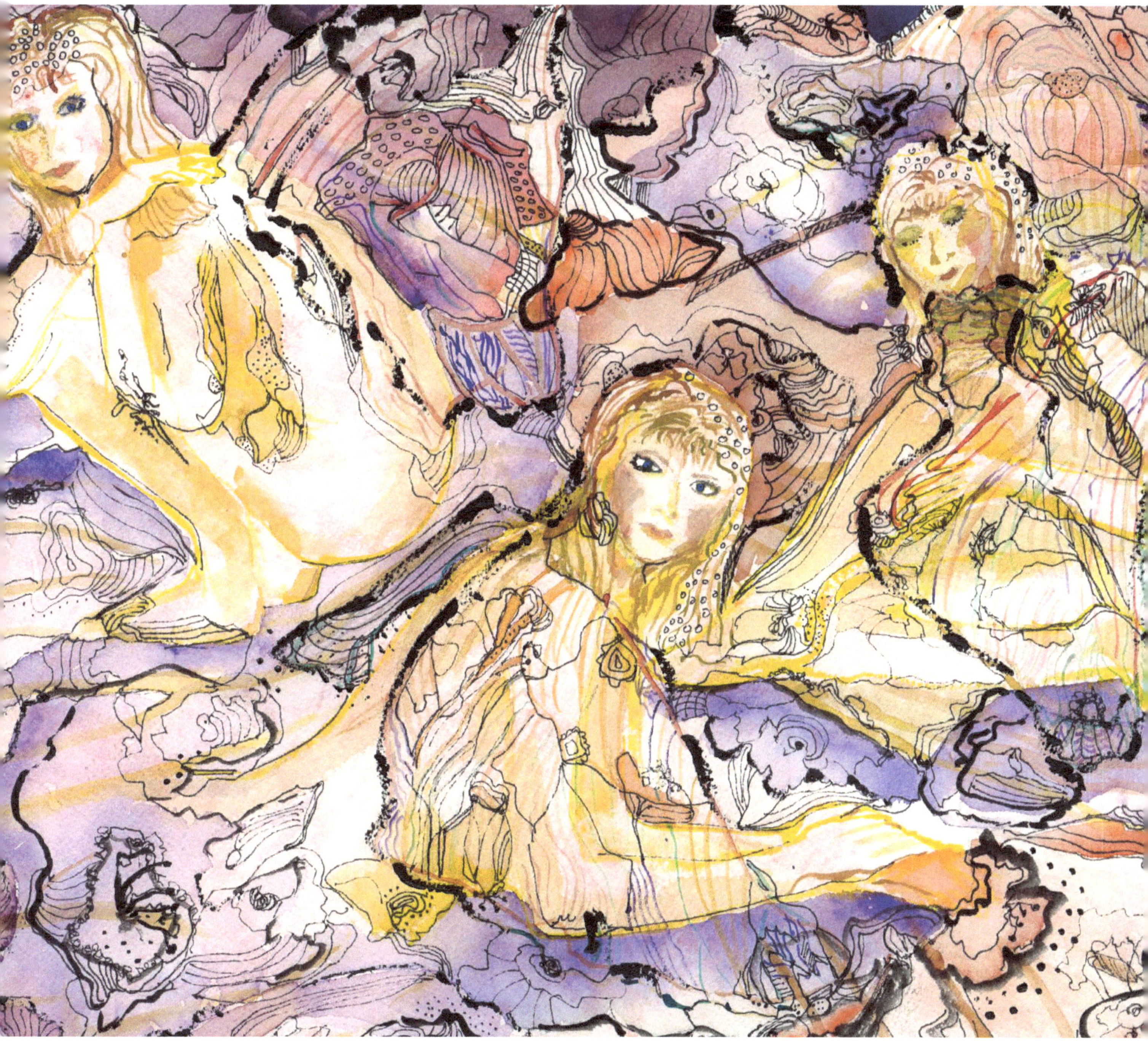

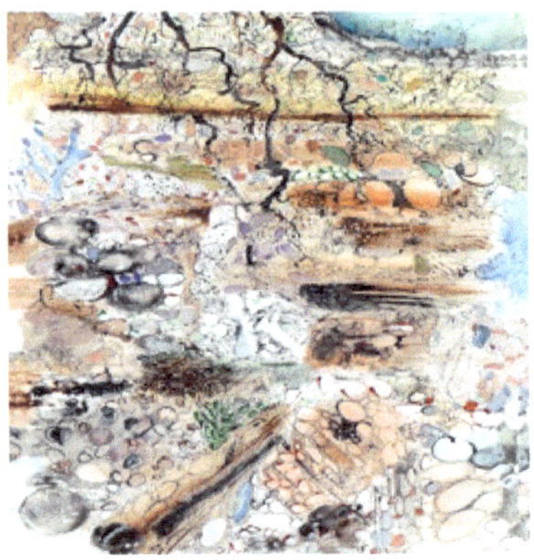

She chose the latter,
springing up through a
compression of regret
and longing, an
impossible bloom arose.
There in its shade she
vowed to love herself as
much as she loved others.

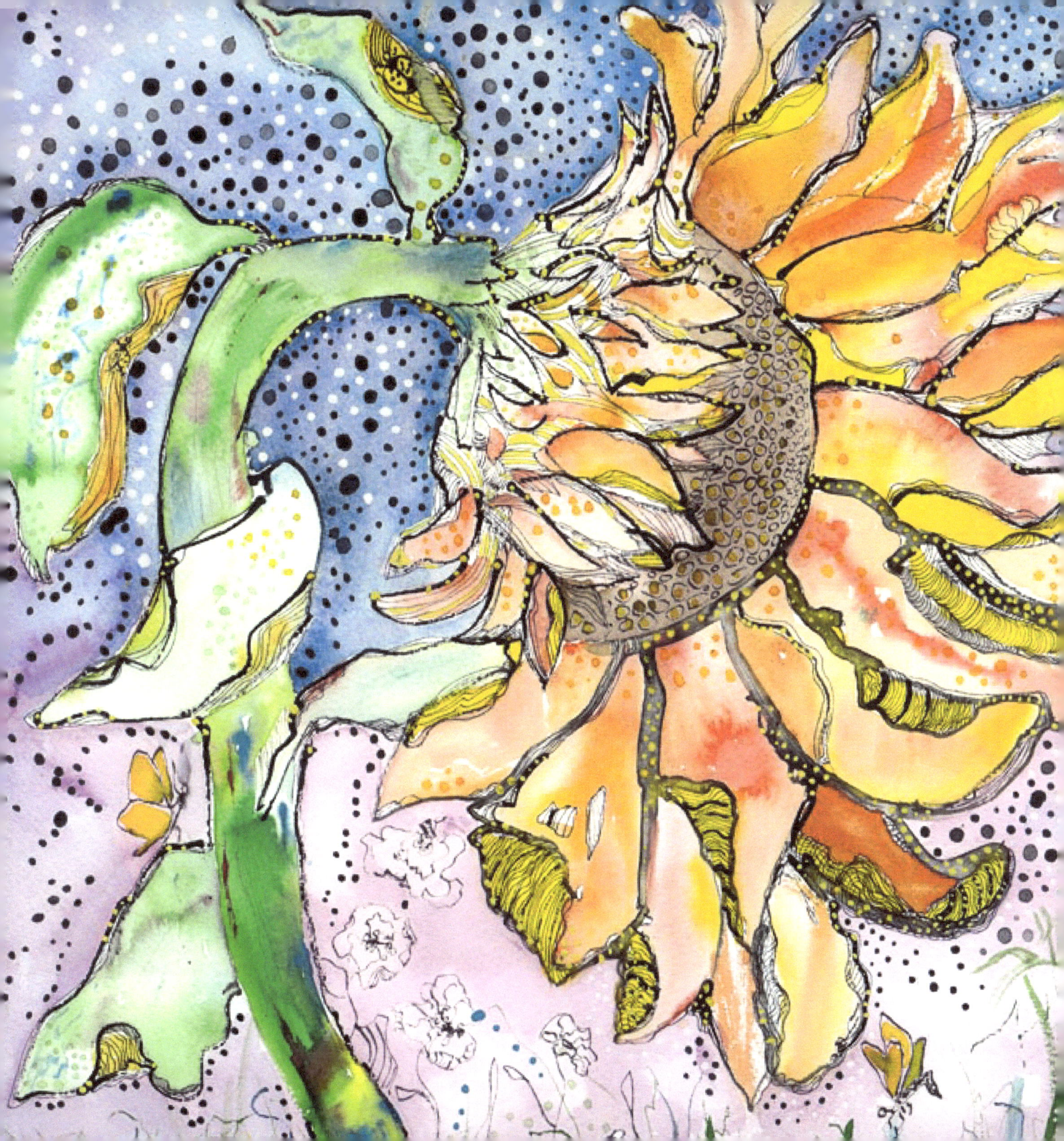

Instantly, rain tested her vow. This rain was not the ilk of thunderheads, but a deluge of what others confused her to be along with the temptation to believe the distortion. Once it erupted, it continued to erupt.

Reckless for freedom, she wove a rope from what had, for long, poorly protected her and urged the blossom of her hidden self upward.

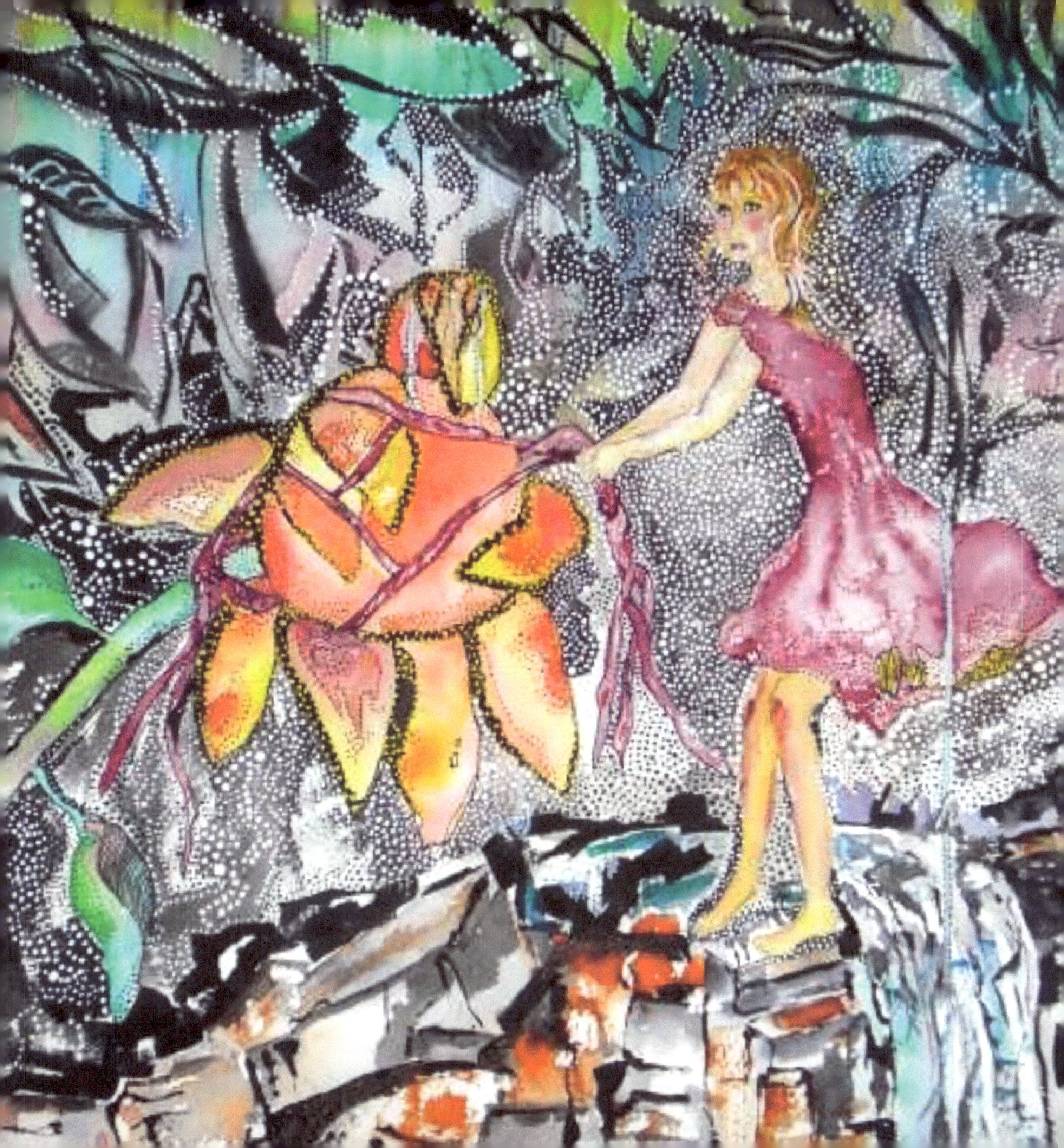

When her strength waned,
she rested, becoming gloriously
small, little to the point of
greatness.

Caught up in the buzz of all she
was not, the sweetness of
pretentiousness ceased.

And she flew and she flew and
she flew and she flew.

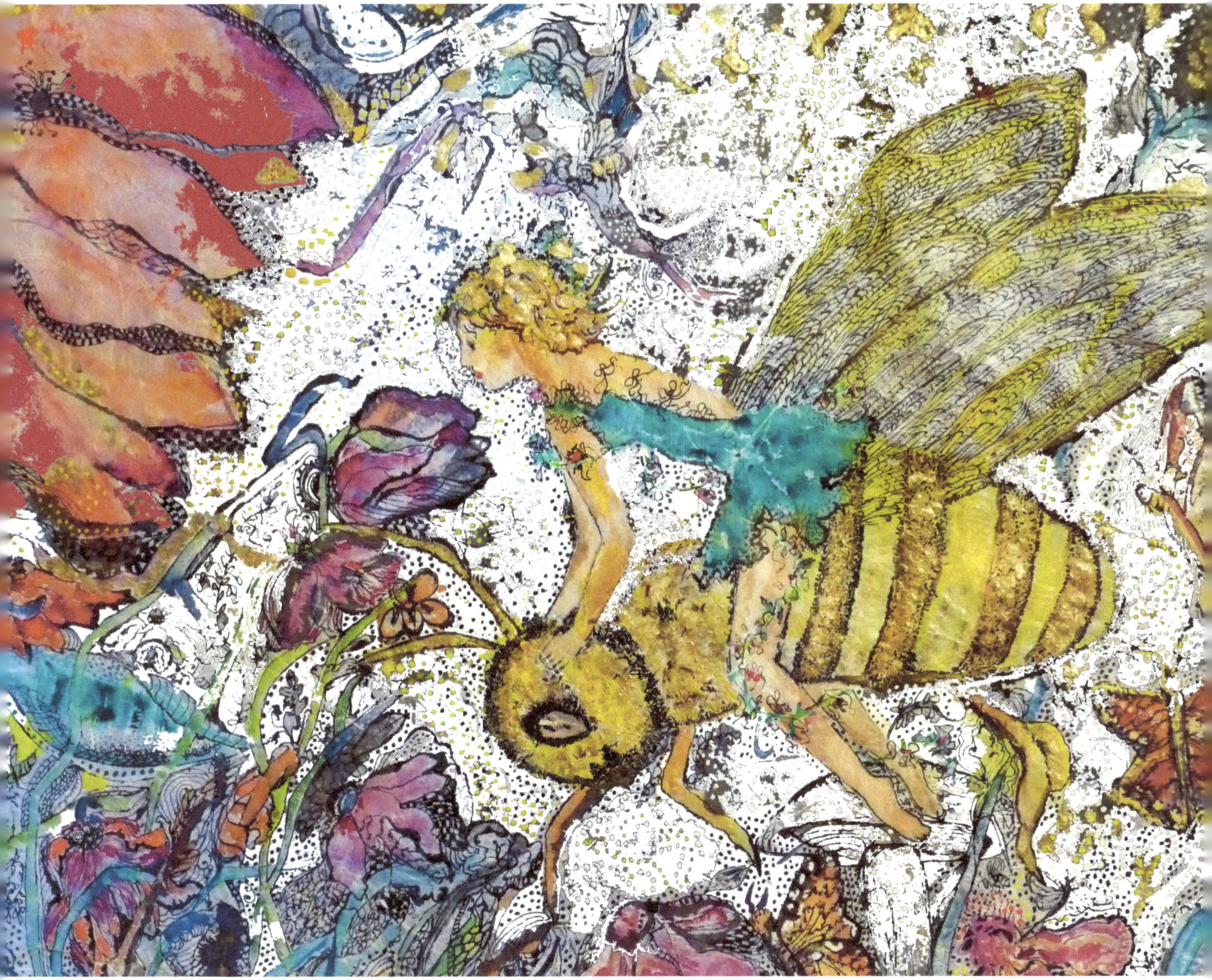

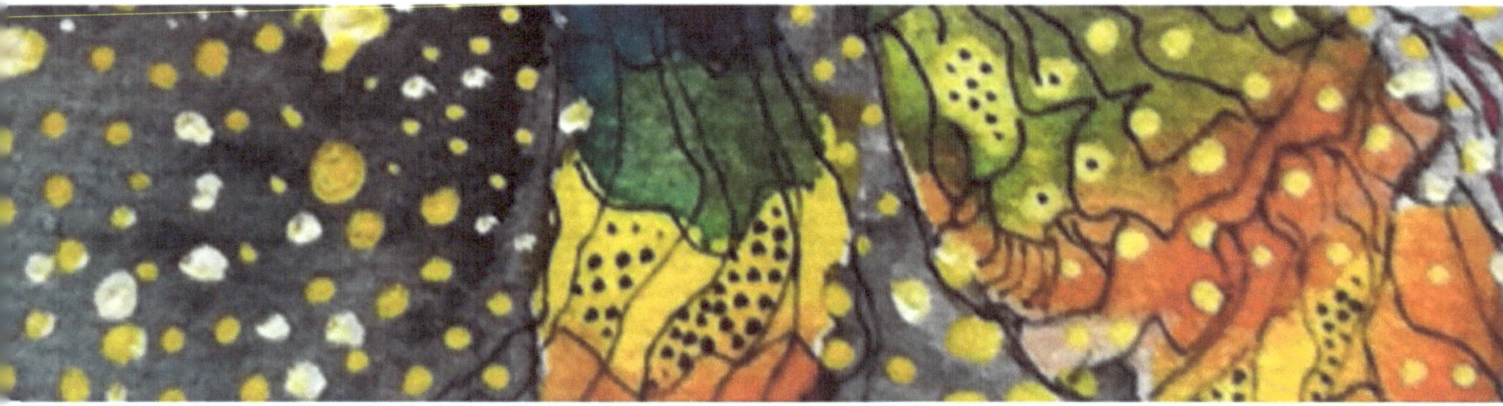

Finally she arrived on holy ground. She threw off her shoes. She stood on tiptoe. She gazed ahead. She glanced behind.

Everything quaked with clarity.

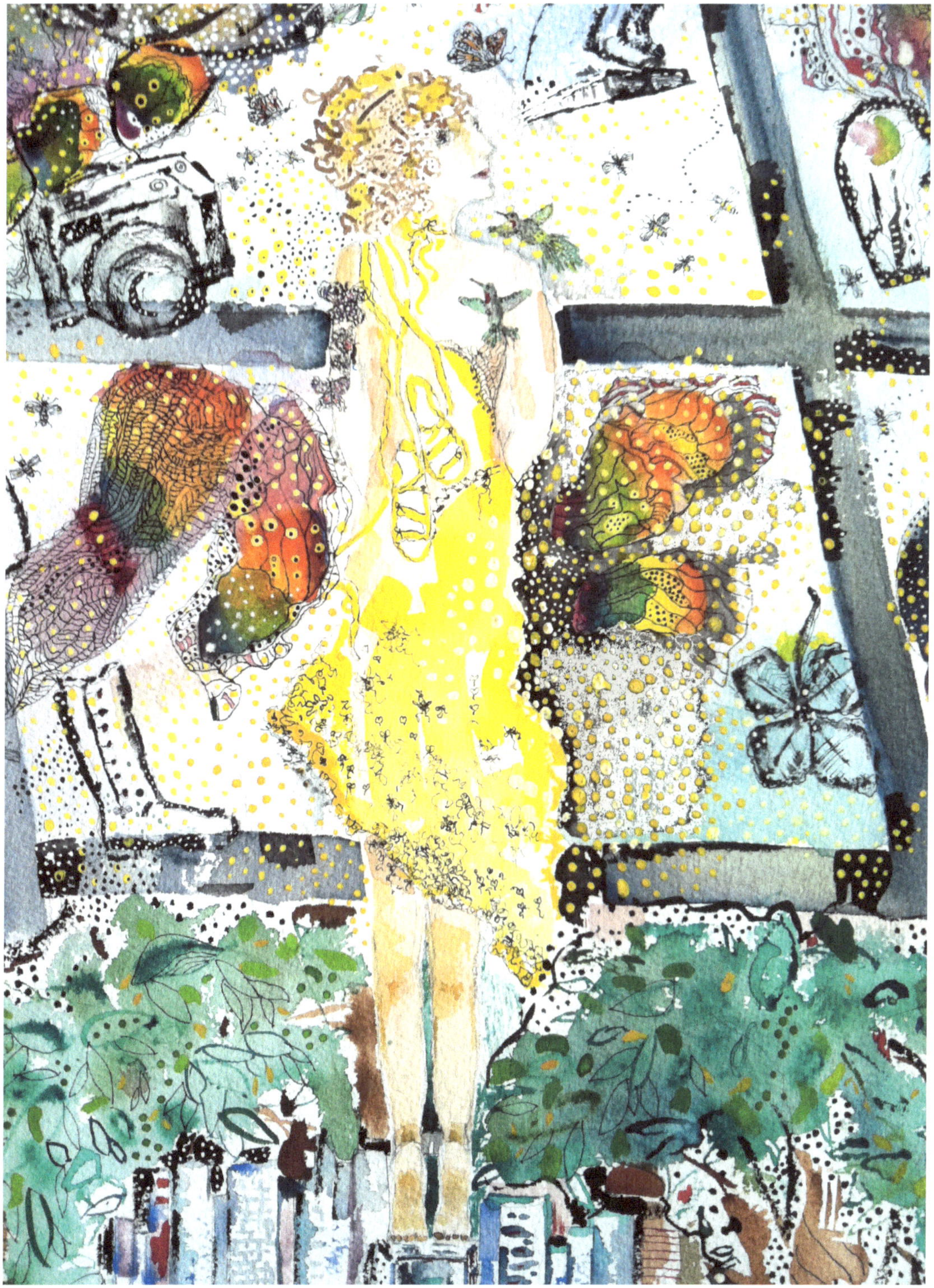

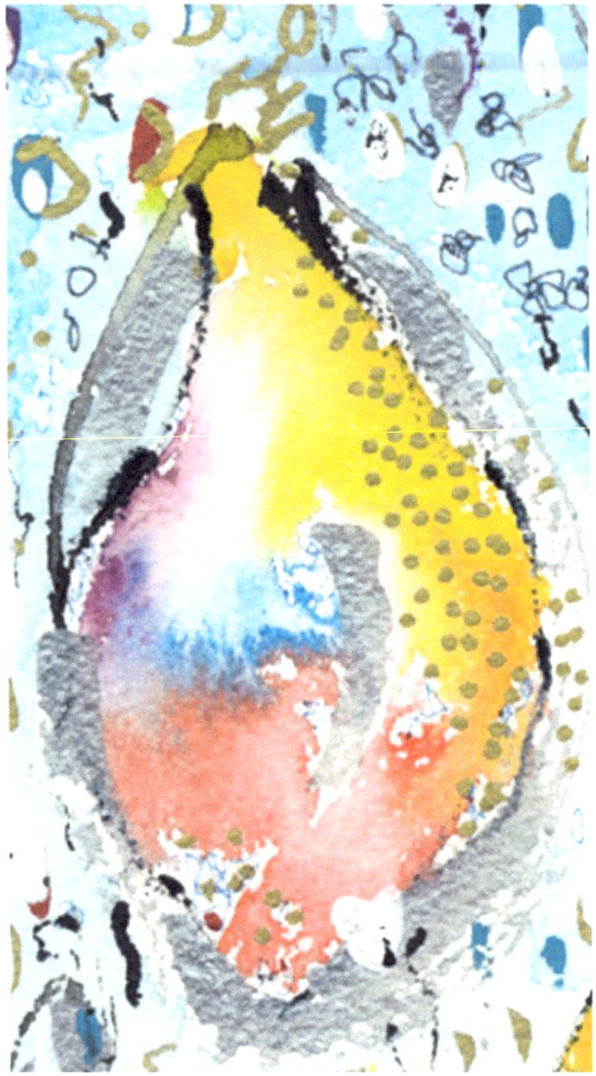

With her arms she made a steeple, with her legs, a harp. Her tears flowed and she opened herself for the harvest.

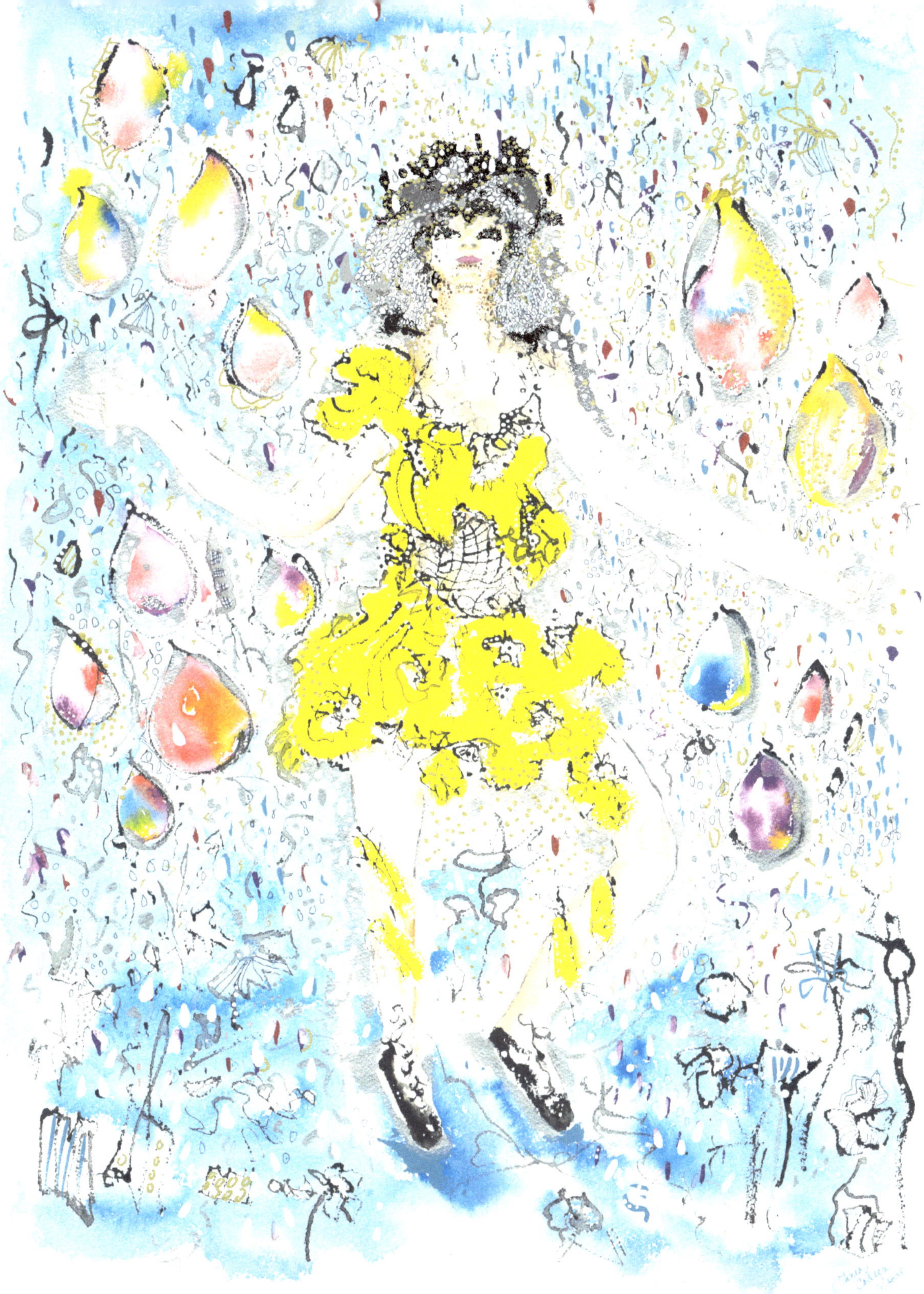

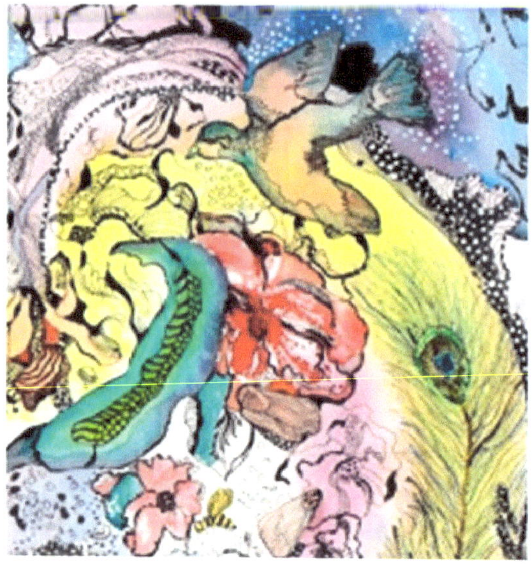

Oh! The music. Such music! An entire symphony performed a song of remembrance.

In a rush of a million wings, a trillion seeds, countless petals and bulging pods, the song sustained her. Out poured the song all waking things remember and all hearing things sing. Not her song but God's song.

The music itself became a ravishing mirror. Gazing into it she remembered long forgotten faces – God's first and then her own.

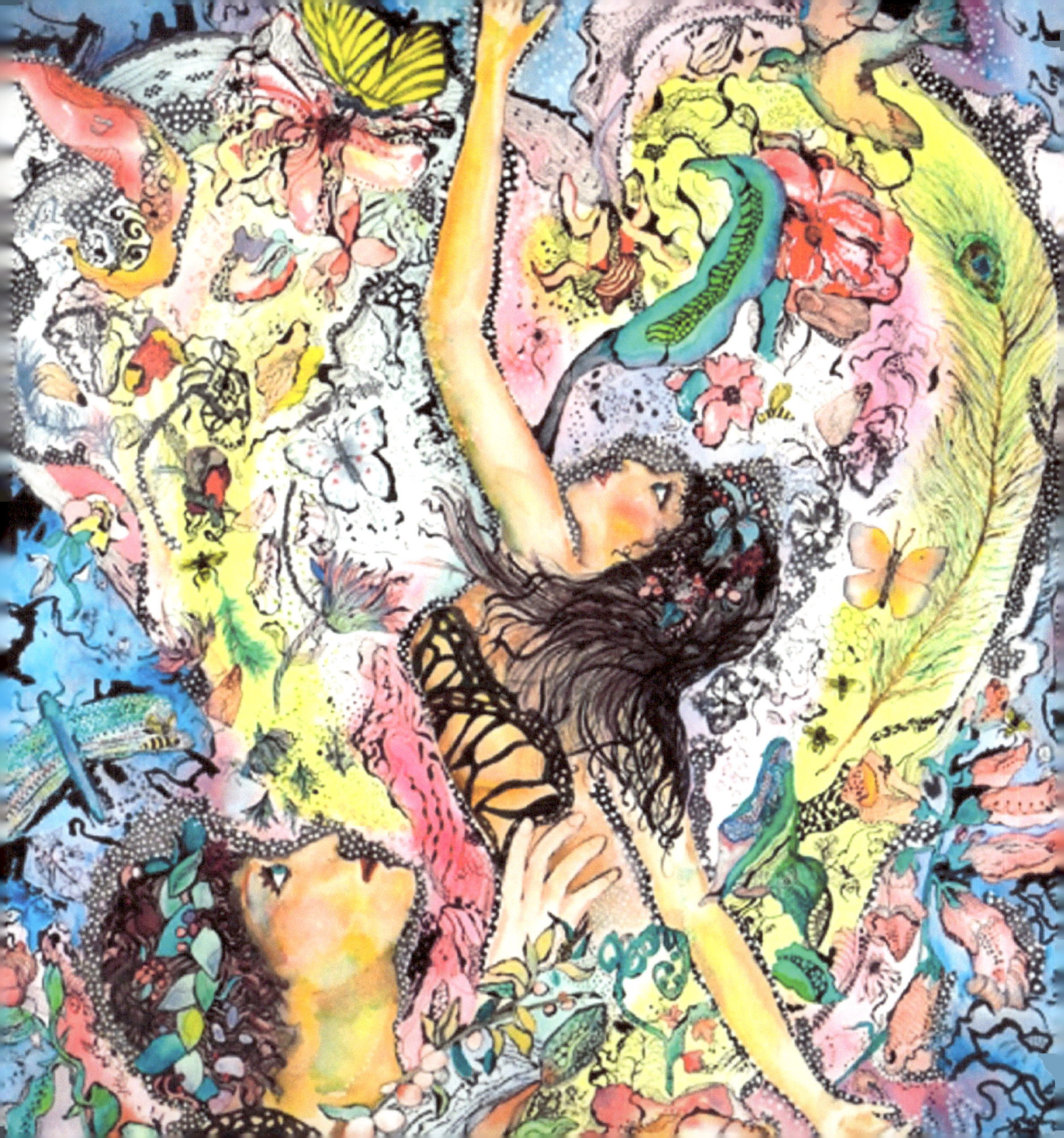

Tonia Colleen Martin

The terrible accident happened too long ago to remember the specifics. Having lost what she doesn't remember owning, it takes the miracle of crossing paths with Hush, Shush and Silence, to reveal the truth. The shock of realizing she struggled to maintain an identity never meant to be hers, floors her. From a position of surrender, the surface of her tears mirrors who she has always been but hasn't seen and does not know. Unimaginable possibilities, surprising choices and thrilling freedom ensues.

At the core of all anxiety is mistaken identity. *About Face* invites readers to consider who they might be apart from other people's expectations and who they might become.

I earned my MFA in Writing from Vermont College of Fine Arts. I write to bear witness to the joys and anguish of becoming more and more human. I believe the love and beauty in our world is not an answer to the deep longing for home, but an arrow pointing to where we were created to dwell once time wraps around itself and eternity unfolds.

My work has appeared in *The Arts in Religious and Theological Studies; Ruminate Magazine, Metonym, Chrysalis* and the *Sierra College Journal. The Color of Grace: Thoughts from a Garden in a Dry Land* was published under a former name by Baker Books.

I have self-published other illustrated adult fairy tale books: *Intents and Purposes; Having Tried Everything; Rest;* and *The String Theory Beginning with Me.*

www.toniacolleenmartin.com
FB: Mining With a Feather

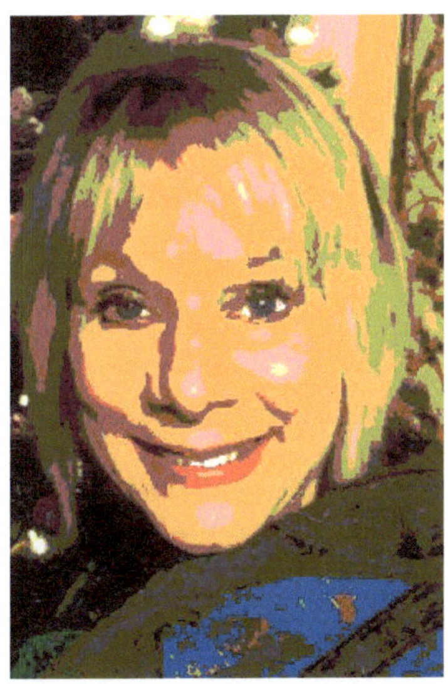

www.ingramcontent.com/pod-product-compliance
Ingram Content Group UK Ltd.
Pitfield, Milton Keynes, MK11 3LW, UK
UKHW061031310726
14089UKWH00009B/188
* 9 7 8 1 0 8 7 8 7 1 5 3 0 *